The Life And Death *of* Beatrice *The Bee*

Brian Haddon

Northern Bee Books

The Life And Death Of Beatrice The Bee
© Brian Haddon

All rights reserved. No part of this publication may be reproduced, stored in a retrieval system, transmitted in any form or by any means electronic, mechanical, including photocopying, recording or otherwise without prior consent of the copyright holders.

ISBN 978-1-908904-53-9

Published by Northern Bee Books, 2014
Scout Bottom Farm
Mytholmroyd
Hebden Bridge HX7 5JS (UK)

Design and artwork: D&P Design and Print

Printed by Lightning Source, UK

The Life And Death *of* Beatrice *The Bee*

Brian Haddon

Northern Bee Books

The Life And Death Of Beatrice The Bee

The Life And Death Of Beatrice The Bee

The Queen Bee woke up ready to start work and was given a good breakfast by her trusted servant bees. The queen set off to find cells in which to lay her eggs. She had a strange feeling that the first egg that she laid today was going to be a bit special.

She found a cell which had been prepared for an egg, and laid the first of many. Three days later a nurse bee put some special food into the cell. The tiny larva emerged from the egg and began to eat the food which was a mixture of pollen and nectar. It tasted very good. Soon the nurse bee came and popped her head into the cell to make sure all was well and to give the larva some more food. Without speaking the nurse bee was able to communicate. "Hello, I shall call you Beatrice. I shall be feeding you for a while." As a larva Beatrice couldn't answer but she ate the food hungrily.

Beatrice, the larva was fed regularly and she grew and grew. After six days the nurse bee made a cap of wax over the top of the cell which made it nice and snug for Beatrice the larva to grow and change into Beatrice the bee.

Becoming a Worker Bee.

When Beatrice had finished growing she just knew it was time to get out of the cell. She began to nibble at the wax lid and, with her head free and a bit of wriggling, she pushed herself out. She was a new bee. It was very noisy but the sound was friendly. She was also reassured by a delicious smell.

As Beatrice stood, a little wobbly, on the comb, feeling around her, the nurse bee came back. Their antennae touched "Well, it's good to see you," said the nurse. "Thanks for your help when I was a baby," signalled Beatrice. "Now it's time for me to help, but first please tell me what that wonderful smell is?" "That's the perfume of the queen, she came by not long ago and the smell goes everywhere she goes. It's wonderful. If you can't smell it there's trouble in the air."

"Now it's time for you to clean out your cell as the Queen may be coming again soon. I'll find out what you'll be doing next."

Beatrice cleaned her cell carefully. It was so dark she couldn't see what she was doing, but all her other senses helped her do the job perfectly.

Beatrice was not a young bee for long. Soon she knew that it was time for her to look after the little ones for a while. She found out which cells held the pollen and nectar and began to feed the new larvae just as she had been fed.

There were bees that had been out of the hive to fetch nectar and pollen, they were called forager bees. Some of them gave Beatrice nectar to feed the larvae, but she took a little for herself.

Beatrice hoped that one day she could be a forager bee and fly away from the darkness. "You must wait your turn," the nurse bee had told her. So Beatrice got on with feeding the larvae which she enjoyed. It was wonderful how quickly they grew. She welcomed them all into the world with a friendly greeting.

In the coming days she did other work. She helped to make new cells, and, for a little while, she helped to feed the queen.

Guarding the Hive.

One day Beatrice knew it was her turn to become a guard for the hive. She found her way down the rows of cells to the bottom of the hive. There she saw the light and walked toward it, soon emerging into the sunlight at the entrance. It was fantastic to be able to use her eyes.

Beatrice was amazed at all the colour, the huge space and all the movement as bees left the hive and others returned from their foraging. The fresh air was invigorating but she was aware that the Queen smell was not outside. Sometimes she went inside to make sure all was well.

There were several guards at the entrance as there were wasps around. If just one wasp got past the guards they would tell other wasps and soon there would be a lot of damage done.

Suddenly there was activity on the hive's landing board outside the entrance. A wasp had pounced on a very tired bee that had just returned from foraging. The bee was stung but still fought back.

Beatrice and three other guards flew to the defence of the bee. Each of them was trying to find a chink in the wasp's hard skin to sting her, even though it meant they would die. More bees came to help. The wasp was fighting back and was able to sting more of the bees but still they fought.

Beatrice stopped trying to sting the wasp and, instead, held on to the wasps wings to make it difficult for her to escape. The wasp was now desperately trying to get away but Beatrice held on. The bees won the battle but three of them had died.

Beatrice was tired after the battle but a forager coming in gave her some nectar and she soon felt better.

It was on the landing board that Beatrice met her first male bee, a drone. He too wanted feeding and tried to push Beatrice out of the way but the forager told him he'd have to wait a minute, only then did she give him some nectar. It was early in the year and the drone was welcome to eat but later he would not be so welcome.

By now Beatrice had learned to clean a cell, feed the babies and the queen, make new cells out of wax, and defend the colony; now it was her turn to stop being a house bee and to become a forager. The need for the colony of bees was to get as much nectar as possible. The larvae would also need pollen.

Learning to be a Forager.

Beatrice stood on the landing board at the front of the hive. She knew that first she had to practice flying and needed to get her sense of direction so that she could return to the hive after a flight. She took off and was immediately aware that it was the sun that gave her a sense of direction. Now she understood the dance on the comb that she had witnessed from foraging bees which told the way to find nectar or pollen. It's called the waggle dance as the bee waggles when pointing in the direction of the food.

The feeling of flying in the open was very exciting but she quickly felt that she must go back and so she turned and flew back to the landing board. She stood there to get her breath back. The mixture of feelings was wonderful.

She took off again and this time flew in a bigger circle before returning. She spent some time practicing, each time going further and further, until she was ready to fly up to three kilometres in search of flowers with nectar and pollen.

The life of the forager bee was hard. Most of Beatrice's life would now be spent collecting nectar and pollen according to the needs of the colony; and the needs of the colony would never end. On the other hand the freedom of flight, the colour of the world of flowers and blossoms never failed to make Beatrice happy. She loved to fly high, over the trees and houses.

Beatrice learned how to understand the dance of the bees. When a forager finds a good place to get lots of nectar or pollen she tells the bees close to her. She does this by giving them a sample of the food she has found and dances over the comb in the shape of a figure eight. The watching bees can tell the direction of the food supply by the way she waggles when in a certain position and also how far away it is.

Beatrice would only collect nectar and/or pollen from one specific flower each time she went out. She swallowed the nectar to carry it but she put the pollen into bags on her back legs.

Danger.

One day Beatrice was approaching a garden with lots of attractive flowers. She was just about to land on one when another bee flew from another flower close by. The other bee was signalling franticly to Beatrice and she followed the bee away from the garden and they both settled on the grass below.

Beatrice realised that the other bee was sick. They touched antennae and Beatrice learned that some gardens were poisonous. The gardener in this garden had used chemicals which hurt bees. It was very sad as Beatrice had to watch the other bee die. She hurried back to the hive to tell the others about the poisonous garden. She hoped that other bees had not been there.

The Swarm.

Beatrice's world was turned upside down one day when the word got around that the colony was to swarm. The queen was going to leave and many of the colony were going to go with her to find more space. They had outgrown the beehive. Beatrice was one of those chosen to leave with the swarm.

Bees in the hive began to build some bigger cells to breed a new queen so that the colony left behind could continue. When the new queen was almost ready the swarming bees began to gather around the front of the hive, all of them had eaten as much honey as they could because they would not have any food in their new home.

They told the queen that they were all ready. She had been on a special diet to make sure that she could fly properly and be fit when they needed her to lay lots of eggs in the new home. When the queen came out the whole swarm took off. It was fantastic; more than ten thousand bees all flying together.

The swarm didn't go far before they came to rest in the upper branches of an apple tree. Beatrice and several other bees left the swarm and flew in different directions. They were scouting for somewhere that would make a new home for the new colony.

In London, where Beatrice lived, there were not too many hollow old trees. She was looking for a similar kind of place with a large space inside for the colony to live in and a small hole that could be easily defended.

Beatrice came across a large garden in Tottenham. There was a hive similar to the one that she had left behind. Beatrice went to it and there were no other bees in sight. She went inside and found it empty. She carefully inspected every corner and when she had judged it be a good place for the colony to live she returned to the swarm.

When Beatrice went back to the swarm she began to make a dance that told other bees what she had found. Soon other scout bees flew to have a look. They agreed with her choice. Although other possible places had been found, the whole swarm was influenced by the enthusiasm of the returning scouts. The place that Beatrice found was chosen and the whole swarm took off and flew directly to their new home.

All the bees, except one. Beatrice was exhausted. She had served the colony well. She found a beautiful blossom, curled up inside and died happy and content.

What you need to know about honey bees.

Except for humans themselves no creatures have been more studied than bees; but one thing that all beekeepers know is that the bees often do not seem to read the same books.

Bees have been on earth for more than 55 million years, Modern Humans for 150,000 years. We need bees more than they need us, because more than a third of the fruit and vegetables that we eat are dependent on plants being pollinated. Some people like to eat meat, which comes from animals. These animals rely on plants to eat. These plants often need to be pollinated by bees.

Bees are dying around the world because farmers and others often forget the need for insects to pollinate the crops. They use poisonous chemicals and cut down a lot of flowering hedgerows and dig up places where wild flowers might grow.

It is very important to remember that we are not doing the bees a favour. They lived before people came and will live after we have gone.

Where Honey Bees live.

Honey bees like to live together in big families. We call them colonies. A long time ago bees lived in hollow trees or on cliffs away from danger. Now, in many countries, they live in bee hives made by people. In the summer a colony in a hive has about 50,000 bees, in the winter about 10,000.

A single honey bee cannot live without the other bees: it is a social animal. Everything the bee does is related to its role in the colony.

People discovered the delights of honey thousands of years ago but usually killed the bees to get it. Now we are able to keep honey bees in a hive and to harvest some of the honey for ourselves, without hurting the bees. It was a beekeeper named Langstroth who worked out that frames separated by a space which was the same as that found in nature would allow frames of honey to be taken without killing the bees.

This Standard National hive has two boxes. The larger box underneath, called a Brood Box, is where there are honeycomb frames where the queen lays her eggs. The upper one, called a Super, is where the bees build their comb to store their honey. The inspection frame is fitted to help inspect the hive by allowing the beekeeper to lift it out of the box.

The Honey Bee.

Like all insects the honey bee has six legs, a head, thorax and abdomen.

All worker bees are female. This is a worker bee. The Honey Bee has two pairs of wings. When they are not folded they hook together for flight.

Bees are covered by fine hairs which are important for spreading pollen from flower to flower when collecting nectar.

The Queen Bee.

There is only one queen bee. Here you see her surrounded by attendant worker bees. A bee-keeper has marked her with blue ink to make it easier to find quickly on an inspection. She is quite different with a much longer abdomen but when there are so many bees she can be difficult to spot.

The Drone.

On this picture you can see worker bees and also three drones, the male bee. Look at the difference in their size and, in particular, the size of their eyes.

The drone does absolutely no work in the hive. He goes around asking the worker bees to give him food. They are normally happy to do this but toward the end of the year they will refuse. His only job is to fertilize a queen when she is on her maiden flight. They do this in the sky where other drones and queens go to mate.

Inside the hive the bees make cells with wax. These are used for larvae to grow, to store pollen and to store honey which you can see at the top left. The honey is fanned so that it evaporates excess water and, when it is perfect honey, a wax lid is put on the cell. Honey from ancient Egypt has been found sealed in this way and it is perfect to eat.

    At the top right of the picture you can see some cells that have tiny eggs laid by the queen. Can you see the queen? Remember the easiest way is to look for the bee which has a body much longer than the folded wings.

    Although all the workers are female there is only one queen. In the picture she is just going to lay an egg in a cell.

    The worker bees gathered around the queen are looking after her. They give her food all day and show her where she can lay her eggs. If they give her more food she will lay more eggs - almost 2000 a day during the busy summer.

The queen will live 2 or 3 years, sometimes longer. The worker bees will only live for about six weeks in the summer as they work so hard. In the winter, when there is less work to do, they live longer.

The queen bee produces a scent, called a pheromone, which tells the bees that everything is alright. If the queen disappears, for any reason, the whole colony knows within an hour and will begin to produce a new queen. If they can't create a new queen the whole colony will die.

Unlike wasps, bumble bees and many other insects, honey bee queens do not hibernate in the winter. When it gets cold the bees cluster around the queen, and any larvae that are developing, to keep warm. The queen does not lay many eggs in the winter. Most other insects die in the winter leaving the queen to start all over again the following spring.

If the bees have not stored enough honey for the winter the beekeeper will feed them with sugar syrup.

The queen bee is the biggest bee in the colony because she has such a large abdomen to carry lots of eggs. The male bee, the drone, is also much larger than the worker bees, he cannot even help guard the hive as he has no sting.

There are hundreds of drones in a hive during the summer compared to tens of thousands of worker bees. At the end of the summer they are no longer welcome in the hive where they eat the precious honey. They are told to leave, even though this means they will die.

The temperature in the hive is very important for the health of the queen and the larva. In the picture you can see a bee which is standing in a particular way so that the draught from its wing beats will push air out of the hive. On the other side of the hive there are other bees driving air into the hive. An air-conditioning system. In the winter the bees cluster around the queen and the larva and shake to make warmth.

Notice the shape of the cell. It is a hexagon, which means it has six sides. It is the best possible shape for the cells as there is no wasted space between them. This shows the intelligence of a colony of bees.

In the bottom of each cell you can see larvae. They are about a week old having come out of the egg after three days. The worker bees are feeding the larvae until they are big enough to become pupae, when they wrap themselves in silk produced from their own body and a wax lid is put on the cell.

Gradually the pupa becomes a fully grown bee. She will eat her way out of the cell, ready start work. The whole process takes 21 days.

There are more larvae in this picture. It is usual for them to have pollen close by. You can see some orange coloured pollen in cells above the brood. Above that is some honey, which the nurse bees mix with the pollen to feed the larvae after they have had royal jelly for a few days.

This mixture is called brood food and is fed to the workers and the drone bees. A new queen larva, in her larger cell, is fed only with royal jelly. She emerges from her queen cell after 18 days. Almost all the other eggs laid become female worker bees.

The top is off the hive for the beekeeper to inspect the bees. He or she only does this when the weather is warm enough, usually above 13 degrees Celsius. The bees normally live in darkness in the hive but they don't seem to mind the light if the beekeeper is gentle.

When you look at the pictures you may have noticed that many of the bees have different markings. They all have the same mother but she will have mated with many different drones and so they can look different.

When she is foraging the honey bee is usually looking for nectar. This is the sugar energy that all living things need. When the bee is going to go a long way for food it only eats enough to get to the source of the food it then takes as much as it can carry back to the colony.

If the colony has lots of larvae it needs pollen as a protein food. The honey bee carries the pollen in bags on her back legs.

One of the many special things about the honey bee is that when she goes to a particular flower to collect food she will only go to the same plant for the rest of the day. This is important for the plant as it helps to pollinate that particular species. 130,000 plant species depend on the honey bee for pollination including one third of the world's food-crops.

It was over 55 million years ago that some wasps became vegetarian. They were the first bees. Wasps are usually coloured black and yellow. They do eat sugar but they also hunt insects, using their sting to kill them. They take the dead insect back to their nest and feed the meat to their babies. The wasp can sting as many times as they want as their stinger is pointed. The worker bee's sting has a jagged end which stays where it stings which means that the bee dies after it has used it's stinger. (If you get stung by accident, remember to look for the sting and scrape it out of your skin or it will continue to pump poison into you). It is only the female bee which stings. The drone has no stinger.

Although the queen produces every egg that becomes an individual bee, it is better to understand the whole colony as the living organism. An individual honey bee cannot survive on it's own.

The bee colony is a wonderful, living thing and we should always try to look after it.

Acknowledgements:-

Anita for introducing me to the world of bees.
The Co-op scheme for enabling me to keep bees myself.
The North London Beekeepers Assoc. for their advice.
My friend Eyad for the photographs.

Thank you for reading the book.

I would appreciate your comments:- brianhaddon@live.co.uk

The Life And Death Of Beatrice The Bee

www.ingramcontent.com/pod-product-compliance
Lightning Source LLC
Chambersburg PA
CBHW081026040426
42444CB00014B/3367